Finding L :
The Great
Alphabet Hunt

Paula Curtis Taylorson

illustrated by Olesya Burina

Finding L : The Great Alphabet Hunt

This is a work of fiction.

Library of Congress Control Number: 2021905026

Printed in the United States of America

A 2 Z Press LLC

PO Box 582

Deleon Springs, FL 32130

bestlittleonlinebookstore.com

sizemore3630@aol.com

440-241-3126

ISBN: 978-1-954191-13-6

Dedication

Thank you to those who read to me and those who listened to me read.

This book belongs to :

_____

It was **late** in the **library** one April day, when three **lovely ladybirds** fluttered this way.

Leaving their garden, they
came **looking** for L clues.

Let's help them **locate** some.
There's no time to **lose**.

Lottie and Lulu and **Lillian** as well,
find **Ls** on the shelves and
have **lots** of stories to tell.

The letters and languages
between the leaves of each book,
bring characters to life on
the lines as we look.

There are **ledgers** and **logbooks**;
some **large** and some small.
Larry the **librarian**,
keeps **lists** of them all.

Larry leaps onto his ladder
and leans to and fro

and goes where **leprechauns live** under R for rainbow!

Larry climbs to
the **level** where
llamas are **loose**,
and they **laze** in
their **loungers**,
drinking
Loganberry juice!

The **ladybirds** feel **lucky** as they **lollygag** through **Lapland** and **Laos**.

and then lightly land one
shelf up on a **lofty lighthouse!**

The **lantern** is **lit**
for those **lost** at sea,

and the **ladybirds** are **launching**
a **lifeboat** rescue party!

Old **Long** John Silver
sits on his **loot**,
eating **lettuce** and **lollipops**
that he keeps in his boot.

On the **lower** shelves,
a **local lion** rules the **land!**
He's **learning Latin**
and **literature** as
he **lays** in the sand!

Litter was left by the leafcutter ants

and the **ladybirds laugh** at a Labrador
wearing **love**-hearts on his pants!

Leatherback turtles
are doing the **limbo**

under some fairy **lights**
leftover from crimbo !

A leopard is lurking in the reference section,

and is **liked** by the **lady** who does book **loan** collection!

Six **lively langoustines** are playing **lacrosse**. The **leader's** a **loud lobster** who says he's the boss!

He yells they're a 'ludicrouslackadaisical' bunch,
So they laughed and light-heartedly
headed for lunch.

The **lemurs** are so **laidback**,
they **lethargically** hang
by their **long**, **luscious** tails
while a **lullaby's** sang.

Some **Lilliputian** people of **limited** size,
leap from a **letterbox** and shout 'surprise!'

Leroy the **locksmith** brought **Lassie** his **lapdog,**

The **loveable** pair
lark about
playing **leapfrog**.

The **lupins** and **lilies** that were trampled, **laid** flat,

Then a **lawyer** came by with a **lavender** hat.

The **lass** that **labels** the
books that are **late**,
Puts on her **lipstick** as she
stands up straight.

Sir **Lancelot** bends down on his
left knee and proposes,

Then, the **librarian locks** up
as the **library** closes.

The **ladybirds line** up,
it's the **least** they can do.
As the L words are safely
locked up for you.

The End

My Very Own 'L' Words:

_____

_____

_____

_____

_____

_____

_____

_____

_____

_____

_____

_____

Glossary

Page 1. **Late** : happening at a time after an expected or usual time, end of the day
Library : a building with many different books for people to take for a short time to read
Lovely : beautiful, pleasant
Ladybirds : flying red insects with black spots, also known as ladybugs
Also on Page 1 : Lemon :

Page 2. **Leaving** - to move or go away from
Looking : to use your eyes to see something or view something, searching here

Page 3. **Let's** - allowing or permitting to do
Locate : find something, see where it is
Lose : to come to be without
Also on Page 3 : **Lamb** : a small farm animal
Lion : a wild animal similar to a cat
Leaf : the flat, irregularly shaped things that grow on trees

Page 4. **Lottie** : a girl or woman's name
Lulu : a girl or woman's name
Lillian : a girl or woman's name
Ls : a letter of the alphabet
Lots : many, to have many

Page 5. **Letters** : alphabet, used to create words or written communication from one person to another
Languages : refers to speech understood by people, communication
Leaves : here - the pages of the book
Life : to bring to real, not dead
Lines : rows of words or other items
Look : to see or understand something

Page 6. **Ledgers** : a place to record transactions
Logbooks : book with details of books lent or payments
Large : big
Larry : a boy or man's name
Librarian : person who works at a library
Lists : series of numbers or other items that makes sense - to do or remember

Page 7. **Leaps** : spring up through the air, jump
Ladder : a structure made of wood or metal with rungs used to walk up and down
Leans : to bend in one direction or another from the straight up and down position

Page 8. **Leprechauns** - dwarf or sprite. Irish folklore
Live : daily activity, a place where one lives, home

Page 9. **Level** : the demarcated area, a certain place, amount of care, the measurement of something
Llamas : a wooly farm animal resembling sheep
Loose : free
Laze : relax, not too much energy
Loungers : chairs
Loganberry : a large dark red fruit

Page 10. **Lucky** : fortunate - good things happen to someone
Lollygag : to go along casually, having fun doing so
Lapland - areas of Norway, Sweden, Finland, Kola Peninsula, countries
Laos - Asian country, South East Asia

Page 11. **Lightly** : in a very gentle way, barely
Land : to settle onto the surface of here
Lofty : floating, carefree, not organized, not realistic - big dreams
Lighthouse : a large tower-like structure/ building with a bright lite for boats and rescue

Page 12. **Lantern** : small portable light
Lit : light, so shines
Lost : can't find their way, stray off course

Page 13. **Lifeboat** : small water craft for rescue
Launching : to set out, beginning a journey or project

Page 14. **Long John Silver** :
Loot : money, treasure, possessions
Lettuce : green leafy vegetable, food
Lollipops : candy

Page 15. **Lower** : situated or found close
to the ground, not tall
Local : nearby, in one area or specific location
Lion : a large wild cat
Land : ground
Learning : to acquire knowledge- information, to
make smarter
Latin : a language
Literature : written work books, letters
Lays : to be situated on the ground or on an object like furniture, recline

Page 16. **Litter** : garbage
Left : to not take with them - remains where they are
Leafcutter ants : ants that shred compost / garbage

Page 17. **Laugh** : to express emotion of happiness and fun
Labrador : large dog from Labrador England
Love : strong, positive emotion

Page 18. **Leatherback turtle** : turtle that does not
have a hard shell, but one made of thick leathery skin
Limbo : a dance

Page 19. **Lights** : brightness to see by
Leftover : not used prior - used portion being used at a later date

Page 20. **Leopard** : a large wild cat
Lurking : concealed, ambush, sneaking around

Page 21. **Liked** : agreeing with something
Lady : a woman or female person who is polite
Loan : give temporarily - expecting back - repay or give back

Page 22. **Lively** : full of pep, vigorous, exciting
Langoustines : a small lobster or large prawn? shimp-like being
Lacrosse : a game
Leader's : the one in charge of the others and what they do
Loud : vvery noisy
Lobster : a sea crustacean

Page 23. **Ludicrouslackadaisical** : made-up word
Laughed : express pleasure, humor
Light-hearted : carefree, cheery, merry
Lunch : a meal in the middle of the say

Page 24. **Lemurs** : a small animal with large eyes
Laid-back : easy going, slow to react, unhurried
Lethargically : lazy, slowly moving, tired, sluggish
Long : not short
Luscious : very pleasing and extravagant - extra special?
Lullaby's : song for babies

Page 25. **Lilliputian** : very small people from Lilliput
Limited : a certain amount only
Leap : jump up suddenly
Letterbox : mail box, box for letters

Page 25. **Leroy** : a boy or man's name
Locksmith : a person who repairs and works
with locks and keys
Lassie : a famous collie dog
Lapdog : a small dog that usually fits comfortably
on a person's lap

Page 26. **Loveable** : attractive, endearing
Lark : flutter like a bird
Leapfrog : a game of jumping over each other

Page 27. **Lupines** : a plant with bright colored flowers
Lilies : flowers
Laid : put or place flat on a surface or the ground

Page 28. **Lawyer** : practices law
Lavender : light purple color

Page 29. **Lass** : a young lady
Labels : a slip of paper, cloth, or other material
to indicate information about an object
Late : after the expected time, over due, not on time
Lipstick : cosmetic to color lips

Page **30. Sir Lancelot** : a legendary character, a knight
Left : opposite of right,
direction of West when facing N

Page 31. **Locks** : a device to secure items or an area

Page 32. **Line** : arrange in a row
Least : smallest or less in size, amount,
less compared to other things
Locked up : secured so no one unwanted
can enter or take

Paula Curtis-Taylorson Lives in Marston Mortaine England. She is a full-time secondary school teacher of English and English Literature. She was amongst the first of the initial students to graduate from the Uk's first BA (Hons) Creative Writing Program at the University of Bedfordshire.

Her first love is poetry and rhyme and she works hard to inspire and teach appreciation of the subject to all age groups. Many of her students have gone on to be successful writers.

www.ingramcontent.com/pod-product-compliance
Lightning Source LLC
Chambersburg PA
CBHW041523120626
46551CB00018B/2545